MEXICOLOR

MEXICOLOR

THE SPIRIT OF MEXICAN DESIGN

PHOTOGRAPHS BY

MELBA LEVICK

TEXT BY

TONY COHAN

CREATIVE DIRECTION BY

MASAKO TAKAHASHI

CHRONICLE BOOKS

SAN FRANCISCO

This book is dedicated with love to my life partner, Hugh,
who shared with me the passionate experience of discovering Mexico.
—M.L.

To my father, Philip Cohan.
—T.C.

To my parents, Tomoye and Henri Takahashi,
who opened my eyes to the world of art and design.
—M.T.

Text © 1998 Tony Cohan
Photographs © 1998 Melba Levick
Photographs © 1998 Masako Takahashi: front cover, bottom left;
p. 13; p. 14, top left and right; p. 15; p. 18, bottom left; p. 52,
left center; p. 60, right; p. 62, right; p. 67; p. 73, top right; p. 79,
top right; p. 82; p. 83; p. 90, left center, top right; p. 97, top right;
p. 114, bottom left, top and bottom right; p. 115, top and bottom
right; p. 126; p. 139, top right; p. 173; p. 176.

Manufactured in China.

Library of Congress Cataloging-in-Publication Data available.

ISBN: 0-8118-1893-4

Cover and book design: Patricia Evangelista
Cover photographs: Melba Levick and Masako Takahashi

Distributed in Canada by Raincoast Books,
9050 Shaughnessy Street
Vancouver BC V6P 6E5

10 9 8

Chronicle Books LLC
85 Second Street
San Francisco, CA 94105

www.chroniclebooks.com

CONTENTS

THE BURNING FLOWER

"Why was I given these hands full of color?" —CARLOS MONSIVAÍS

COLOR IS EVERYWHERE IN MEXICO. Street and market, food and dress, home and garden are suffused with it. Green of cactus, lime, cornstalk. Red of tomato, watermelon, bullfighter's cape. Yellow of corn, *cerveza*, sunflower…

The colors come from nature, and from history. The Mexican painter Rufino Tamayo liked to point out that his pigments were drawn from the world around him, colors people see and use in their lives. Blue of indigo, water, sky. Orange of mango, purple of eggplant, white of plaster wall…

Sometimes the colors appear in arresting, even startling combinations. A green pickup truck passes by, brimming with bright orange marigold blossoms, food for chickens so the yolks of their eggs are a deeper yellow. Purple bougainvillea tumbles over a black wrought iron balcony against an eroding yellow wall, revealing layers of color beneath—traces of history and the passage of time. A woman in a turquoise blouse and red shawl, a bucket of pink roses on her head, pauses to look at riotously colored folk toys (*juguetes*) colliding on a market seller's blanket—a perfect example of what the Mexican writer Octavio Paz calls "the fiesta of the object."

In Mexico, every color goes with every other color—if you know how to do it. It is this "adventure of disorder" (in artist Chucho Reyes' words) that determines the color in a striped *serape*, a Mexican kitchen, a market seller's arrangement of multicolored plastic buckets. What counts is not abstract color theory but living affinities and relations. The Mexican architect Luis Barragán, when asked why color was the dominant element in his work, responded, "For the sheer pleasure of using and enjoying it!"

Brown of adobe, chocolate, coffee. Pink of conch, hibiscus, flamingo. The sun's gold is an Aztec calendar, a church icon, a brass band in the plaza. A silver ingot from a Guanajuato mine is Taxco jewelry, a bayonet, fish scales…

ABOVE: Flowers in a patio of the Hotel Camino Real, Oaxaca. *OPPOSITE:* Row of brightly colored houses in Guanajuato.

ABOVE: Exterior of Frida Khalo's house; two Oaxacan women in huipiles. BELOW: Colorful boats of the Xochimilco Floating Gardens.

Part of this visual affluence stems from Mexicans' comfort with the idea of chance, luck, fortune. The *lotería* and other such games of luck still thrive in Mexico. At some point, human effort must surrender before the capriciousness of fate, which may reveal the divine. "Chance," the Mexican writer Gabriel Zaid has said, "is another name for God." So colors freely combined become, in a sense, "an attempt to… give God a chance to intervene in my life."

Visual color echoes a sense of color in all things. *Sabor, sonido, salsa, sensación.* Taste, sound, flavor, sensation. Mexican speech is rich with expletives and words of affection. This sensory profusion is understood to show generosity of heart and imagination (as opposed to—even in defiance of—the pinched, merely functional esthetic many Mexicans feel rules the country to the North).

Sometimes color carries quite exact meanings. The Puebla dish *chiles en nogada*—green chiles, red pomegranate seeds, white sauce—transforms the colors of the national flag into a seasonal delicacy, coinciding with September's patriotic festivities. Village walls or houses are painted a deep matte blue, *azul añil,* to protect against evil spirits. The richly colored woven *huipiles* (sleeveless tunics) worn by Mayan women bear information on village, rank, economic position, age, marital status, and occasion.

A strip of blue water, *agua azul,* glimpsed through green palms. A *licuado* (juice) stand proffering fat glass jars of papaya orange, *horchata* (almond drink) white, watermelon red, *limón* green, pineapple yellow…

Color also comments on its absence. The very sun that in Juan Rulfo's famed novel *Pedro Páramo* "glowed on the stones, lit everything up with color" can also (in the same novel) burn, wither, and destroy. Mexican life can be harsh, severe: scarcity stalks the land, crops fail, rivers dry up, children and animals die. Abundance is not to be taken for granted but celebrated. So color brings relief from the parched earth—the renewal of crops, water and life, birth and celebration: fiesta. The Huichol, people of peyote and the dry desert, chant: *For we are all/children of a flower/a flower of brilliant color/a burning flower…*

So the color that floods Mexico's streets and plazas, markets and homes (and the pages of this book) is language and metaphor—a form of communication, deeply bound to experience. Day and night, birth and death, rich and poor, feast and famine: color is always there. Earth, sky, and history conspire to make it so.

> *"When I use a strong color like red or purple, it is because
> my mind has suddenly been illuminated by the memory of some Mexican festival,
> some stall in some market, the brilliance of a fruit, a watermelon, or a wooden house…
> This is timeless architecture which will never outlive its period
> because it belongs to no period…"* —LUIS BARRAGÁN

The contemporary traveler in Mexico—artist, tourist, anthropologist—marvels at the bright yellow-orange *flor de calabaza,* or squash blossom, both flower and food. Savoring it in a taco or as a soup, she may not realize that recent discoveries in a cave in Oaxaca place

an agrarian society in southern Mexico as early as 8000 B.C., contiguous with comparable societies in China and the Middle East, and that evidence included human bones, and the rind and seeds of that same yellow-orange *calabaza*. Color, it would seem, was part of the Mexican mix from early on.

Ancient Mexico's massive stone monuments and ruins were resplendently polychromatic inside and out. The vast structures of the Toltec city of Teotihuacán (200 B.C. to A.D. 750), the Zapotec tomb walls of Oaxaca's Monte Albán, the Mayan temple complex of Palenque, were all painted with vivid exterior colors. Inside, frescoes employed red, turquoise, ocher, orange, green, white, yellow, black—colors very much in use in Mexico today. The Templo Mayor, in present-day downtown Mexico City, exhibited "rich, brilliant and perfectly clear" colors, according to the first European chroniclers: cerulean blue, yellow, red, orange, ocher, black. Mayan murals were often painted in deep greens with black backgrounds, dark-red and pink-red details, yellow-and-black leopard skin capes, and garments of so-called "Maya blue" (whose enduring pigment qualities still remain mysterious).

Weaving was extant in Mexico as early as 5000 B.C., with fruits, flowers, leaves, and bark all serving as dyes. The deep-red dye produced by the cochineal insect, which feeds on cacti, was (and is) used to color garments; so were sea snails gathered along the Pacific coast that produced a delicate lavender. Countless other plants and inorganic substances—iron oxide, gypsum, ocher (and, of course, gold and silver)—provided a lavish color palate. A contemporary visitor to the National Museum of Anthropology's pre-Hispanic collection sees jade carvings, gold statuary, Toltec clay figures covered with mother-of-pearl mosaic, obsidian-glaze ceramics, and funerary masks encrusted with turquoise, serpentine, and shell.

From the beginning, color was entwined with Mexican public ceremony and private adornment, religious temple and home. The vibrant clothing, customs, and crafts markets that still abound in many areas of Mexico today, especially among its nearly sixty surviving Indian tribal groups, are a direct link to that resplendent pre-Conquest world the painter Diego Rivera attempted to celebrate in his ambitious, sprawling murals in Mexico City's National Palace.

For three centuries after the arrival of the Europeans—roughly 1520 to 1820—colonial Spain mined and shipped Mexico's arts and resources back to Europe. "I have seen the things which were brought to the King from the new golden land..." wrote the great German artist Albrecht Dürer in 1520. "A sun all of gold... and a moon all of silver... and all manner of marvelous things for many uses...I saw among them wonderful works of art, and I marveled at the subtle genius of men in distant lands." Exotic foods, plants, and herbs—corn, squash, chocolate, tomato, potato, *cacao* (coffee), *chicle* (gum), tobacco—flooded into Europe, rapidly and permanently transforming tastes. "The new lands," wrote Octavio Paz, "appeared as an unknown dimension of reality... the visible revelation... of invisible powers."

Meanwhile the influence of local cultures in the "new lands" was brutally suppressed. Friars and governors, eager to stamp out "undesirable" traits, banned forms of personal adornment such as face and body painting. Non-Indians were forbidden to wear Indian cos-

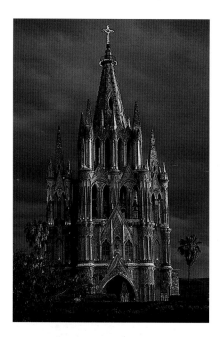

tume styles. At every turn the dour Spanish oligarchy and the morbid inclinations of the Inquisition conspired in favor of the somber. It was as if color itself had become subversive.

Yet vital new arts were forged out of conquest and the collision of cultures. European glazing techniques combined with local materials produced a thriving ceramics industry in the city of Puebla. Treadle-loom techniques taught at the missions blended with indigenous weaving and embroidery styles. Cloth imported from Europe, and later the Philippines and China, were worked into fanciful Mexican shawls and other new garments. Ornate polychrome Indian decorations and frescoes depicting local and Christian deities adorned Catholic missions and churches, as old and new gods made way for each other.

The overthrow of Spanish rule from 1810 to 1821 triggered the release of color back into life. The effulgent imagery of the Virgin of Guadalupe, vivid *retablos* (devotional paintings on tin), and a resurgence of native color in everyday life were inseparable from the new Mexican nationalism. The Revolution of 1910–1920—an attempt to redistribute land and wealth—was drenched in color: blood, propaganda posters, the new flag. When it was over, the Mexican contemporary period began in earnest.

After a brief flirtation with the cool, severe Bauhaus International Style, Mexican artists turned to their roots for inspiration. Spearheaded by the architect Luis Barragán, the artist and anthropologist Miguel Covarrubias, the painters Diego Rivera and Frida Kahlo, and enthused visiting artists (photographers Edward Weston and Tina Modotti, filmmaker Sergei Eisenstein, among others), a new-found pride in "Mexicanness" kindled a vigorous efflorescence in the arts: rich colors, playful spirit, robust native energy. Painters took up muralism; composers and writers and dancers looked to the pre-Hispanic, the folkloric; anthropologists and ethnologists eagerly plumbed the mysteries of ancient Indian cultures. A national textile industry began, blending old techniques with synthetic dyes imported from Europe and Asia. The charismatic Frida Kahlo championed indigenous clothing and wore it exclusively: the woven sash, the handwoven skirt, the *huipil*, the *quechquemitl* (cape), the *rebozo* (rectangular fringed shawl). The great haciendas, mostly destroyed during the revolution, came back to life as inns, restaurants, and museums.

As Mexico discovered itself, the contemporary world was discovering Mexico. Before and during World War II, European Surrealists came to Mexico as to an artistic Lourdes. Spanish film director Luis Buñuel took up residence in Mexico and made many films there, as the American John Huston did. A new generation of Mexican architects and designers introduced bright, colorful innovations into the contemporary home. Mexico became (and remains) a site of artistic and spiritual renewal for voyagers from every corner of world.

In recent decades, Mexico has had to meet the challenge of economic setbacks, political turmoil, and assaults from a global consumer culture. Along the coasts and in the cities, overpopulation and tourism tax the ecosystem. Many distinctive materials used for arts and crafts have disappeared or are in short supply: *amate* bark paper, cochineal dye, the *aje* grease used in Michoacán lacquerware. Each year in the markets at the time of the Day of the Dead, there are more Halloween masks and fewer hand-decorated sugar skulls. The all-purpose *rebozo* is as often seen in museum collections these days as wrapped around women's shoulders.

Yet miraculously the unique Mexican sense of color in all things survives. Ceramics, lacquerware, baskets, textiles, and metal, glass, wood, and stone work have so far outlasted the onslaught of contemporary goods. Though sales of factory cloth and ready-made garments grow, indigenous styles remain in use 450 years after the Conquest, especially in rural areas. A visit to any of Mexico's state-run Fonart stores will reward the collector with examples of beautiful handcrafted folk art gathered from all parts of Mexico. Mexican street life, religious processions, and home life still bear the colorful, seemingly indomitable spirit of *alegría* (joy).

Internationally, Mexican influence has never been stronger. Cooking delicacies from every region of Mexico now share the menu with the *taco, enchilada,* and *tamale* in Paris, New York, and Tokyo restaurants. Mexican architecture, design, and home furnishings are an integral part of the international vocabulary of style. Traveling museum exhibitions regularly show Mexican arts and artifacts in the world's capitals, and Mexican artists command large prices on the international market. The color-drenched apparition of Frida Kahlo has become a global icon.

"Why was I given these hands full of color?" asks the contemporary Mexican writer Carlos Monsiváis. It is a rueful, ironic question, full of deep mystery. Where does the color come from? Genetic inheritance? History? God? Is it a blessing or a curse, to have these hands full of color?

One answer to Monsiváis' questions is beyond doubt. The unique Mexican relationship to color—inspired, intrinsic, inseparable from life itself—is alive in the Mexican spirit today. It sings forth from every page of *Mexicolor*.

—TONY COHAN, MEXICO, 1997

BELOW: Mayan cape from Chiapas; carved wood armadillo from Oaxaca.

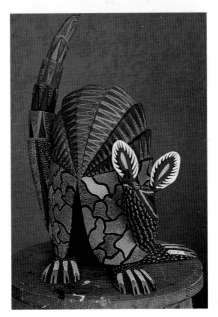

CHAPTER

1

THE PAINTED WALL

THE MEXICAN WALL IS AN ENIGMA.

It keeps things out (people, animals, dust, floodwater) and in (secrets, posses-sions, people, animals). It divides but doesn't conquer. It separates while uniting. ❁ The wall is like clothing—a layer or barrier demarcating public and private space. Combining three formal cultures, it guards the interior, the Mexican "labyrinth of solitude" (in Octavio Paz' famed phrase). The urge to see behind, over, or through it creates mystery and interest. ❁ The Mexican wall may be of *adobe* (mud and straw), stone, brick, or wood. It may be covered with a layer of cement (*aplanado*), or not. Traditionally, the surface is painted with a slaked lime whitewash known as *cal*, simply left white or mixed with colors. ❁ Though some regions favor certain colors (Michoacán's white upper walls with red borders below) or certain tones (Guanajuato's pink or pistachio green limestone from local quarries), walls tend to be as variously (and richly) colored as the tastes or expressions of their owners. ❁ Life happens to the wall. Dogs use it. Sellers squat against it. Teenagers embrace against it. Plants affix themselves to it. The seasons etch their message across its face. The wall is repainted—again and again—laying new color over old, further embedding its secrets. ❁

ABOVE: A magenta-painted mesquite door serves as an entry to a lavender blue house. *OPPOSITE:* A row of houses on the Costa Carreyes.

ABOVE AND OPPOSITE: Doors and windows inset in brilliantly colored Mexican walls, which appear in endless shades of color, often within the same wall, changing with the light and the weather. Traditionally, *cal* (slaked lime whitewash) is tinted with powdered pigments; salt and cooked nopal cactus juice are sometimes added for extra adherence. The various color treatments worked out of these simple materials enliven every Mexican community's private and public walls. The surfaces quickly erode, obliging frequent repainting—an opportunity to paint the house another color, perhaps. When a new layer flakes off in spots, previous colors are revealed.

LEFT: Cool greens and blues endow a room in coastal Puerto Vallarta with an almost Matisse-like charm. *OPPOSITE, TOP AND BOTTOM LEFT:* Warm colors lend an intimate, comfortable feeling to a *casita* in a Mexican mountain inn. *OPPOSITE, TOP RIGHT:* Soothing rose-colored walls and simple rustic furnishings create a relaxed atmosphere in a beautifully restored colonial courtyard. *OPPOSITE, BOTTOM RIGHT:* Bright yellow walls transform a long narrow entrance and stairway into a cheerful gallery and showcase.

17

OPPOSITE, TOP LEFT: Donkeys bearing bags of potting soil pause before a warm, reddish wall in the central mountain town of San Miguel de Allende. During fall or winter, the same donkeys may deliver firewood from door to door. OPPOSITE, BOTTOM LEFT: A pair of handmade brooms, still used for street sweeping in Mexico, stand in the bright sunlight against a low brick-red cement wall. LEFT: Oaxacan women make their way to market, their blue aprons blending in with the cool blue wall behind them. ABOVE: A festive array of hanging potted plants stands in relief against an intense blue wall.

CHAPTER

2

TILES

SKILLED CERAMISTS ARRIVED FROM
Spain soon after the conquest of Mexico, bringing Arabic and European enamel glazing techniques and the potter's wheel. They settled in the town of Puebla, and soon a flowering of tilework and ceramics began. ❀ At first only European patterns were copied, using the Talavera technique (named after the Spanish town of Talavera de la Reina where the style originated), employing a tin-glazed white clay mixture. Hand painted blue and white *azulejo* tiles predominated, though other colors were used. Tilework spread rapidly throughout colonial Mexico, in public structures and in colonial homes. Church domes, private gardens and stairways, patios, kitchens, and bathrooms—few surfaces were without the bright, decorative Puebla tiles. ❀ The Talavera tradition continues today, a theme with many variations (so much so that since March 17, 1995, the date of an official declaration, only ceramics following the strict sixteenth-century formulas have the right to use the term "Talavera"). The *azulejo's* square still poses a compositional challenge Mexican artisans respond to with endless innovation. In recent decades the town of Dolores Hidalgo in Mexico's *bajío* region has come to rival Puebla as a major ceramics manufacturing center. ❀ Though its origins lie in the distant past—in Persia, the Arab world, Delft, Italy, Spain, China—Mexican tilework is today considered unique to the country: a "chosen skin," as the writer Alberto Ruy-Sánchez Lacy puts it. ❀

ABOVE: Though multicolored tilework is ever more common in Mexico, traditional blue and white tiles remain much in use. The hummingbird is a symbol of love. *OPPOSITE:* Rows of geometric tiles decorate the risers of a stairway in the Casa de la Marquesa Hotel, a restored colonial mansion in Querétaro that features Talavera tile throughout.

ABOVE, TOP: One of Mexico City's great historic buildings, the Casa de los Azulejos (The House of Tiles) has been restored several times since its construction in the sixteenth century. It has survived earthquakes, murders, explosions, and has even been the site of a declared miracle. *ABOVE:* A view of the upstairs offers a sense of the building's rich ornamentation. *TOP, RIGHT:* A fountain in the main dining room combines elaborate stone detailing with a mixture of tilework. Formerly a colonial mansion and now a popular restaurant (Sanborn's), the entire structure inside and out is a showcase of Puebla tilework. *RIGHT:* View of the completely tiled exterior.

OPPOSITE: A section of tile mural bordering the corridor overlooking the main dining room of the Casa de los Azulejos combines floral and figurative elements, in blue, green, yellow, and red.

ABOVE: This hanging ceramic wall decoration comes from a workshop in Dolores Hidalgo. *OPPOSITE:* Many tile patterns were used to make the charming breakfast nook in this private home. All are from Dolores Hidalgo, a thriving tile and Talavera-style pottery center in north-central Mexico.

LEFT: A densely tiled yellow and green bathroom, accented with Talavera-style planters and clay candle holders designed by the late Herón Martínez of Acatlán, Puebla. *BELOW*: A gaily colored basin combined with hand-painted tiles lends warm colors to a guest bathroom. *OPPOSITE, TOP LEFT*: A bathroom sink made of leftover tiles blends geometric and pictorial *azulejos* into a whimsical whole. *OPPOSITE, TOP RIGHT*: A restaurant bathroom in Valenciana, outside the city of Guanajuato. The ceramic sink enlivens the carved stone pedestal with a burst of color. The restaurant, located in a former hacienda, also sells ceramics and other folk crafts. *OPPOSITE, BOTTOM*: Elaborate design and exquisite tilework distinguish this bathroom in Cuernavaca. The majolica column adds an unusual touch.

CHAPTER

3

LA COCINA

[The Kitchen]

ALL OF LIFE CONVERGES IN THE
Mexican kitchen. Every art and craft can be found there: woven baskets from
the market, large clay *ollas* (cooking pots) for making beans, handblown glassware, tin canisters, carved wooden spoons, chocolate whisks, pre-Hispanic
metates (stone mortars and pestles). ❀ Fresh flowers, foods, and herbs arrive regularly, bought in the markets or from door-to-door sellers. Bright tile counter-
tops and wood tables overflow with green, red, and yellow *chiles*, white onions,
orange squash blossoms, blue corn *tortillas*. Bouquets of gladioli, native tuberoses,
and roses fill colorfully decorated ceramic vases. Pungent sauces bubble in
enameled pots, while meats and vegetables sizzle on the *comal* (grill). ❀ The
Mexican kitchen is a creative site, repository of magic and lore. Women con-
verse and console, nurse and raise children, sort out family matters in *la cocina*.
Love affairs and revolutions are hatched (as in Laura Esquivel's best-selling
book and film *"Como Agua Para Chocolate"*—"Like Water for Chocolate") in the
kitchen. ❀ A Mexican kitchen may be in a home or in a restaurant—in Mexico
or elsewhere. It may be in an elegant hotel, or on a local street corner under an
improvised awning, serving *atole* (warm corn drink), *tamales*, succulent *tacos* or
cochinita pibil (Yucatan-style pork) to a loyal populace every night. ❀ Wherever
it is found, *la cocina* is the warm center, the heart that feeds the extremities. ❀

ABOVE: A graceful handcarved swan, made
in the state of Mexico, holds a collection
of wooden spoons and chocolate mixers.
These mixers, whose origins lie in pre-
Hispanic times (chocolate is native to
Mexico), are twirled between the palms
of the hands to make a frothy chocolate
drink. *OPPOSITE:* An extravagant mixture of
color and pattern characterize the Puebla
Talavera tilework in this Cuernavaca
kitchen. Designed with the modern con-
veniences, the kitchen still retains a traditional Mexican feeling.

ABOVE: This charming kitchen, done in a rustic style, suits its owner, a writer of children's stories and a Mayan scholar. The bowls above the fire hood are hand-painted by Estéban Valdez, a potter from Pantoja, Guanajuato, whose work is in the Smithsonian collection.
RIGHT: Unglazed fire bricks provide a bed for the wood-fire cooking area in this kitchen. Cooking fires are made on three large stones, symbolizing three maidens prominent in Mayan lore.

LEFT: In this contemporary Oaxacan kitchen, brick-toned tilework on walls, counter, and floor establishes a neutral tone against which bright flowers, fruit, and other food stand out. Notice the built-in *comal* (grill) in the corner. BELOW: Richly colorful tiles are used to make a cooktop in this intimate kitchen. Both tiles and cookware are from Dolores Hidalgo.

LEFT: An effusive collection of local pottery and wooden accessories decorates a Oaxacan artist's kitchen. Colorful pots are stored conveniently on the wall. ABOVE: Red chiles in a turquoise enamel bowl add color to an already colorful kitchen. Metal utensils hang alongside pottery on the wall. A common interlocking geometric pattern (Arabic in origin) of deep blue and yellow diagonal tile is used on the counter and the splash-back.

LEFT: Haciendas were virtual communities in themselves, and needed huge kitchens. This one at the Hacienda San Gabriel Las Palmas near Cuernavaca features an unusual horseshoe-shaped serving/cooking area, designed to accommodate several cooks at once. *ABOVE:* A fondness for folk art is the hallmark of this kitchen. Vintage *retablos* (ex-voto paintings on tin) decorate the wall above the sink. The floral printed oilcloth is a typical Mexican print. Tiles from Dolores Hidalgo decorate the walls, sinks, and counters.

4

CASA QUINTA QUEBRADA

THE SIXTEENTH-CENTURY COLONIAL town of San Miguel de Allende lies three hours north of Mexico City in the central highlands known as the *bajío*. Like Cuernavaca and Lake Chapala before it, it has found favor with foreigners in recent decades, especially North Americans. A community of artists, professionals, and retirees has grown up there, supplemented by weekend and holiday visitors from Mexico City. ❋ A number of interesting homes have been restored or built in San Miguel in recent years. The Casa Quinta Quebrada, built by Texans Elton and Martha Hyder, is one of the earliest and most elaborated examples. In 1959 the Hyders purchased an old property on a sloping hill a few blocks below the town center. It took a year to renovate the existing house. Over the next thirty years, the Hyders bought adjacent properties, adding a pool and other structures. In 1988, with the assistance of Mexican designer Patricia O'Gorman and Texans Chris Hill and Marsha Brown, they began enlarging the property. The present work was completed in 1991. ❋ Today the Casa Quinta Quebrada is a beautifully designed and landscaped hillside estate with ten bedrooms, eleven bathrooms, four kitchens, several guest rooms, and servants' quarters. In spite of its size, it manages to provide a warm, welcoming atmosphere. ❋

ABOVE: A weathered green *trastero* (dish rack) stands in front of deep rose–toned walls near the kitchen. *OPPOSITE:* From a balustrade of potted geraniums, guests can glimpse the dome of the nearby nunnery, La Concepción, beyond the lavender flowers of the jacaranda tree.

LEFT: The second-story living/dining area is replete with fireplace and views of the lavish grounds. Antiques from around the world mix with upholstered *equipal* (leather and wood) seating from Guadalajara. The coloration of the walls unites the old and new additions. *BELOW:* Table is set for *comida* (midday lunch). Handblown glass, Talavera plates, and napkins are all Mexican. The antique leather chairs are Spanish colonial-style.

ABOVE: The poolside living/dining area outside the original living room. Large green pottery pieces from the state of Michoacán lend color and texture. *OPPOSITE, TOP:* A corridor, planted with clivia and philodendrons, sports a *charro* (cowboy) motif. Vintage items from former haciendas cover the walls. Bedrooms open onto the corridor and the courtyard, all part of the original house. *OPPOSITE, BOTTOM:* The warm orange tone of the wall, the deep green of the shade-loving plants, and the rustic bench with its hand-loomed cotton cushions make this shaded corridor an inviting place to rest.

LEFT: Deeply textured, the Casa Quinta Quebrada is full of romantic detail. The intimate dining room is filled with blue and white ceramics from Puebla and Dolores Hidalgo, handwrought accessories, and colorful tiles. *ABOVE:* An outdoor living area near the pool. The colored walls and yellow cushion fabrics help soften the massiveness of the stone wall. An *ojo*, or eye-shaped window common in colonial architecture, is set into the wall.

ABOVE: Rows of antique copper pots hang from *vigas* (beams) in the main kitchen. The deep, hand-hammered pots—the same designs brought over from Spain in colonial times—are made to this day with very little change in the village of Santa Clara del Cobre in Michoacán. *OPPOSITE:* A kitchen, one of four in Quinta Quebrada, designed to encompass two work areas: the cooking and cleanup area, and a prep room (behind the stove), which has a table and chairs, storage cabinets, and a breakfast nook.

CHAPTER

5

TEXTILES

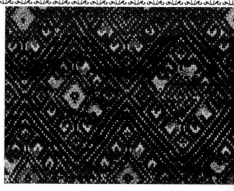

LEGENDS SPEAK OF A MARVELOUS age before Columbus, during the Toltec reign of Quetzalcóatl, when cotton grew in many colors. Certainly weaving was extant in Mexico by 5000 B.C., with fruits, flowers, insects, leaves, and bark all serving as dyes. The conqueror Cortés marveled at the dyeing and weaving artistry in the cotton textiles Montezuma gave him, and spoke of the "variety and the naturalness of the colors." ❀ Europeans introduced the shirt, trouser, blouse, and *serape*. At the missions, Indian men were taught treadle-loom weaving. Cloth imported from Europe, and later Asia, was combined with Indian cloth. After the Revolution a national textile industry was begun. ❀ Today in Mexico, cotton and acrylic are rapidly replacing silk and wool. Indigenous textiles are falling out of use and into museum collections, while synthetic dyes, thread, and ready-made garments fill the markets at an alarming speed. Yet in rural areas and in the south of Mexico, many still wear the traditional *huipil* (embroidered women's tunic), *quechquemitl* (closed-shoulder cape), and *rebozo* (long, narrow cloth with knotting and fringe at each end) every day, not just on ceremonial occasions. Indian-run cooperatives such as Sna Jolobil in Chiapas keep the dyeing and weaving arts alive and locally controlled. Happily, folk art stores in Mexico and throughout the world continue to offer traditional Mexican textiles to the discerning shopper or collector. ❀

ABOVE: Detail of a typical *huipil* from the Mayan community of San Andrés Larrainzar, Chiapas. Red, black, yellow, and white are associated with the cardinal points. Blue stands for the Maya. *OPPOSITE:* Hanks of hand-dyed, homespun wool are ready for weaving at the workshop of Eulalia García de Martínez in Teotitlan del Valle, Oaxaca. Like many other Zapotec weaving workshops in this village known for its rugs, this one is family-run, its techniques passed from generation to generation.

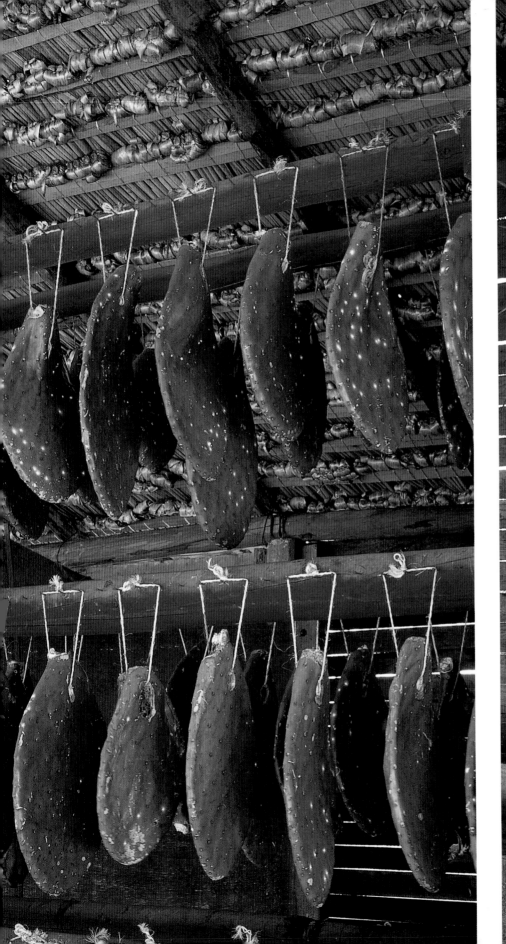

FAR LEFT: Hanging *nopal* cactus are the cochineal bugs' feeding grounds. When crushed, the insect exudes a dye, which becomes shades of red. The insects are sun-dried or toasted on griddles then ground to a powder and mixed with alum, lime juice, or salt. Wool and silk are extremely receptive to this form of dye. CENTER: A lidded pot of dye with wooden dippers hanging above. Slatted walls leave room for air to circulate. LEFT: In the traditional method, yarn is dipped in large pottery jars full of dye. The number of immersions determines the depth of color.

LEFT: After the sheep are sheared, their wool is first washed then carded (combed out) to prepare it for spinning into yarn. Vegetable dyes continue to be used to color the yarns, though commercial dyes are more common. *BELOW:* Maestro Isaac Vasquez G. sits at his footloom in Teotitlan del Valle. His workshop specializes in the use of natural dyes, including cochineal, an insect dye much coveted in Europe after the Conquest. *RIGHT:* Traditional Zapotec designs from the workshop of prize-winning master weaver Arnulfo Mendoza, on display at La Mano Mágica gallery in Oaxaca.

LEFT, TOP TO BOTTOM: Detail of a beribboned *huipil* (woman's tunic) from San Andrés Chicahuaxtla, Oaxaca; detail of an Amusgo cotton *huipil* from Xochislahuaca; a close-up of embroidered embellishments on a Zinacantec cape. *ABOVE:* Satin-stitched embroidery from San Pablito, Puebla. *BELOW:* Detail of a Chinanteco *huipil* from San Lucas Ouilán, Oaxaca. *OPPOSITE:* Two Zapotec women from Oaxaca dressed in traditional *huipiles*. *OVERLEAF:* Two traditionally dressed women from Pátzcuaro, Michoacán. The black-and-blue striped *rebozo* shawl is typical of the area. The intricately cross-stitch embroidered aprons cover minutely pleated full skirts; A private collection of *huipiles* from different regions of Oaxaca. Traditionally, a woman's village, age, rank, and marital status are identified by the pattern of her *huipil*; embroidered dresses from San Juan Chilateca, Oaxaca. Colored, commercially woven fabrics are hand-embroidered with tiny flowers around the yoke and sleeves.

ABOVE: Young women dressed up for the crafts fair held every year on Palm Sunday in Uruapan, Michoacán. Some of the finest examples of folk art from the region are on display and sold at the fair. Note the sumptuous black and blue cotton *rebozo* trimmed in red and orange rayon macrame. Necklaces and embroidered white blouses are worn on top, velvet and lace below. *RIGHT:* The spring solstice is celebrated by pre-Colonial-era festivities in Santa Clara del Cobre, the copperware-making town in Michoacán. Festive floral and ribbon headdresses are worn for special processions. *OPPOSITE:* Children are decked out for a day at the Uruápan Palm Sunday folk art extravaganza. Child-sized native costumes include a blue-and-black striped *rebozo*, and velvet- and chenille-embroidered blouse and apron.

CHAPTER

6

FOLK ART, TOYS & SKELETONS

IN AN OFT-TOLD ANECDOTE, THE

Mexican artist Frida Kahlo, visiting Paris with her painter husband Diego Rivera, found Europe's vaunted drawing-room surrealism dull compared to the everyday surrealism of Mexican life. Indeed, when Surrealism's founder André Breton arrived in Mexico in 1938, he was astounded by the extravagant juxta-position of the fanciful with the improbable everywhere he looked, and wrote ecstatically about it. ❀ Nowhere is this "surreal" quality more artfully evident than in Mexico's wildly imaginative, fanciful folk toys (*juguetes*) and "magical-realism" assemblages of clay, wood, metal—or any material at hand. Always bright and playful, they run the gamut from simple tops and board games to visionary depictions of heaven and hell that rival Dante's *Divine Comedy*. ❀ Mexican attitudes toward death incorporate a playful morbidity, and each year, as the Day of the Dead approaches in early November, the markets brim with skulls (*calaveras*), skeletons, and images from the afterlife, done variously in ceramic, *papier mâché*, wood—even sugar. The recent incursion of commercial Halloween masks from the North, with its competing ritual of *triquitrit* (trick or treat) threatens the survival of these handmade fantasies that so artfully trans-form grief into laughter. ❀

ABOVE: Death and devils are treated with whimsy in Mexican toy-making. Clay, wood, and *papier mâché* are common materials. This assemblage of riotous skele-tons, *diablos* (devils), and other folk objects reminds us to enjoy life while it lasts. *OPPO-SITE: Papier mâché* dolls have been made for generations in the town of Celaya. Colorful decorative items, they come in sizes from a few inches to two feet tall. Their arms and legs are made separately and tied on so they can be stood up or seated.

ABOVE: Animated clay chickens are characteristic of the work of Candelario Medrano from Santa Cruz de las Huertas, Jalisco. Brightly painted, they appear to be singing. *RIGHT:* A handcarved toss-toy and a noisemaker decorated with *lotería* (lottery) cards. Old-fashioned toys like these are still available in traditional markets such as Mercado Libertad in Guadalajara, and in arts and crafts shops.

BELOW: A life-sized ceramic Oaxacan *danzante* (dancer). Because of its height and weight, it is made in three sections. BELOW, BOTTOM: *Papier mâché* maestro Jesús Aguilar from Celaya made this ornately garbed, two-foot-high *china poblana* (named after a Chinese woman who supposedly once lived in Puebla and dressed in this manner. Through the years she has taken on the colors of the Mexican flag, and wears a sombrero).

61

ABOVE: A fanciful unglazed candleholder painted in cheerful naïve colors. Birds, also made of clay, are attached by wire, adding a dainty air; serpents, humans, and *alebrijes* (imaginary creatures) ascend this Ocumicho "tree of life." *RIGHT:* A merry collection of Mexican folk art and textiles, exhibiting what Mexican writer Octavio Paz calls "the fiesta of the object."

FAR LEFT: A whimsical ceramic church made by the Medrano family of Santa Cruz de las Huertas, Jalisco. The Medranos are known for their delightful renditions of churches, circus scenes, apartment buildings, trains, boats, and other enchanting scenes from everyday life. *LEFT:* A phantasmagorical Ocumicho creation. *BELOW:* This imaginative depiction of Adam and Eve in the Garden surrounded by angels was made in Ocumicho, Michoacán.

ABOVE, TOP: Clay skeleton toys made in Guanajuato for the annual Day of the Dead holiday on November 2. The painted skulls in the bowl are made in two parts, with a separate lower jaw joined by a string through the skull. Pull the string up and down and the jaw opens and closes, making the skeleton appear to laugh or talk. *ABOVE:* A painted clay Last Supper from the village of Ocumicho brings levity to a frequently depicted scene. Here, each *sombrero*-topped diner is a skeleton. *RIGHT:* A Tree of Life populated with skeletons, made by the Castillo family of Izúcar de Matamoros, Puebla. Skeleton imagery increases near the yearly Day of the Dead holidays, when families pause to commune with their departed and invite them back to earth.

LEFT: A life-sized articulated skeleton, seated on a bench, carved by Estéban Medina from San Pedro Ixtlahuaca in the Oaxaca valley. *BELOW:* A Ferris wheel full of skeletons, turned with a crank. This fantastic *juguete* (folk toy) is made by the Manuel Gómez Rosas family, one of the last surviving traditional toy-making families in the city of Oaxaca. *BELOW, BOTTOM:* In this painted miniature, a skeleton mother gives birth to a skeleton baby with the aid of a skeleton doctor. Colorful, imaginative clay miniatures from Amozoc, Puebla, depicting every imaginable human drama, are sold in select markets and folk art stores around the country.

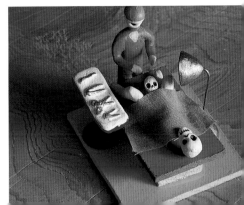

CHAPTER

7

CERAMICS

MEXICAN CERAMIC ARTISTRY IS FED by two great tributaries, the indigenous and the European. Pottery is generally considered to be the greatest of all pre-Hispanic arts and crafts—taught by the god Quetzalcóatl, it was said, "so clay might fly like a bird" (writer Ernesto Cardenal). Every day Mexican farmers' plows and roadworkers' pickaxes turn up hundreds of shards from the ancient past. ❀ The Europeans brought glazing, the potter's wheel, lacquers, and new shapes. For several centuries the Spanish-derived Talavera ware and low-fire native ceramics remained separate—by edict. Both survived—indeed, flourished—separately, and later in combination. ❀ Today ceramics is the most widely practiced craft in Mexico. Every state of the republic works in clay. The diversity is dazzling, both in kind and in technique—from the functional to the ornamental to the sheer fantastical; from single-fired earthenware—brush decorated, burnished, polychrome—to twice-fired glazed chinaware; from the master artisans of Oaxaca to the high-volume producers of Dolores Hidalgo. New forms arise constantly as modern materials simplify work, consumer needs shift, clay becomes available (or, sadly, not), and each generation of ceramists evolves its own innovations. ❀ Mexico remains, as before, a land of potters. ❀

ABOVE: Jars made in wood-fired kilns in Cocucho, Michoacán come in all sizes. The blackened marks are from smoke and occur randomly in the firing process. *OPPO-SITE:* A potter forms a vessel on a wheel in the workshop of Guanajuato ceramist Gorky González. González combines wood-fire techniques he learned in Japan with traditional Talavera colors and patterns.

ABOVE: This potter at the Gorky González workshop is so adept that each large pot, though completely done by hand, is uniform in dimension. **LEFT:** A potter, surrounded by finished pieces and works in progress at the Gorky González workshop, paints a pot in one of the yellow, green, blue, and red patterns the workshop is known for.

ABOVE: Dolores Hidalgo in the state of Guanajuato is a historic colonial town devoted to the production of ceramics and tile making. A young woman in the workshop of Juan Vásquez paints a huge vessel, which, when done, will look similar to the minutely detailed one in the foreground.

LEFT: A corner of a salesroom at the Vázquez workshop displays urns, flower pots, and other ceramic objects. As in most other workshops in Dolores Hidalgo or Puebla, artisans produce ceramics ranging in size and complexity from tiny cream pitchers to entire fountains and murals. *BELOW:* A complicated polychrome ginger jar made in Dolores Hidalgo sits in a colorfully painted *nicho* (niche). *Nichos* are commonly inset in church walls, public areas, and homes, providing an opportunity to display flowers, sculpture, or sacred objects.

71

LEFT: Soft-toned fish designs in brown, on cream-colored pottery from Tzintzuntzan, Michoacán. *BELOW, LEFT TO RIGHT:* A hand-formed religious figure, La Soledad, stands in front of contemporary decorative dishes made in Atzompa, Oaxaca, at the Adelina Maldonado workshop; green-glazed cup, bowl, and candelabras demonstrate the expertise of potters from the village of Patambán, Michoacán; pots from Patambán. The pineapple is made in San José de Gracia, and the pieces with bird motifs are from Patamban, made by Ayunga Suárez Neftali.

ABOVE: Two covered ginger jars in a traditional zigzag blue and white Talavera-style pattern. RIGHT: An angel candleholder made by Navidad Peña of Tzintzuntzan, a large platter painted by Esteban Valdez of Pantojo, Guanajuato, and a decorative vessel by the late Herón Martínez, of Acatlán, Puebla. FAR RIGHT, TOP TO BOTTOM: Typical low-fire coffee, chocolate, or *atole* (warm corn drink) mugs from Tonalá, Jalisco; depictions of local scenes from everyday life are the signature of naïve pottery from Tzintzuntzan, a village near Lake Pátzcuaro in Michoacán; green-glazed lizards rest on unglazed pottery from Dolores Hidalgo, Guanajuato, echoed by the green cast-iron lizards in the foreground.

FAR LEFT: A collection of unglazed pottery from San Bártolo Coyotepec, Oaxaca. The black color results from the manner of firing in the wood-burning kilns, the sheen from burnishing with a quartz stone before firing. LEFT: Maestro Valente Nieto, son of the late Doña Rosa Real de Nieto of San Bártolo, demonstrates making a pot on his pre-Hispanic wheel, which consists of two inverted bowls. It was Doña Rosa who first burnished her pots to create a smooth shiny surface. BELOW: Three women carry black pottery typical of San Bártolo Coyotepec. The village is an important pottery center in the valley of Oaxaca. Doña Rosa's son and grandchildren carry on her work, which is renowned in Mexico and abroad.

FOUR ARTISTS' HOMES

A OAXACAN PAINTER, A EUROPE-BORN
Mexican artist, an American sculptor and his Mexican artist wife, a celebrated
American photographer. Each has responded to Mexican color and mystery with
a home rich in personal vision. Rodolfo Morales' playful, color-drenched rooms
echo his painting palette, while Pedro Friedeberg's witty sculptures and paintings combine with his extensive collection of others' work to literally furnish his
hillside home. Painter Ana Pellicer and sculptor James Metcalf have turned
both house and workshop in Santa Clara del Cobre into a celebration of copper's
possibilities, while renowned art and fashion photographer Deborah Turbeville
has transformed an old colonial home into a site of intense personal fantasy. ❀

ABOVE: A view of internationally acclaimed
artist Rodolfo Morales's color-rich Oaxaca
City studio. The veteran painter and
muralist has exhibited widely throughout
the world. *OPPOSITE:* Morales's abundant pictorial imagery is reflected in his home. In
this richly outfitted kitchen, pictures on the
doors, painted by Morales, play tantaliz-
ingly with the theme of food. Functional
pottery from the area, clay jars, and cooking pots of every size cover the walls.
Countertop and wall tiles reflect colors
prominent in Morales's paintings.

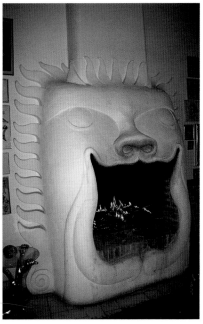

OPPOSITE: The sitting room at Mexican artist Pedro Friedeberg's San Miguel de Allende home is filled from floor to ceiling with art and artifacts, as well as paintings and furnishings of his own design. The bright red bookcases hold a large collection of *santos* (saints), old toys, and various *objets d'art*. ABOVE: Pedro Friedeberg is widely known for his surreal paintings, drawings, and sculpture. Here, a fireplace he designed in the form of a laughing monster (inspired by the Bomarzo estate in Italy) stands next to his unique, handcarved "King Midas Table," with its gold-leafed feet and hands. *LEFT, TOP AND BOTTOM:* A dining area opening onto a small central courtyard of the Friedeberg house. The melon-colored walls create a sense of warmth and sunlight, though the corner is often in shade. The mirrored standing screen reflects the unicorn table the artist designed; the *entrada* (entry) is filled with hats, *retablos* (votive paintings on tin), primitive Coptic paintings, and paintings by Friedeberg's wife, Carmen Gutiérrez.

ABOVE: Metcalf's sculptures and Ana Pellicer's work highlight their white-walled living room. All of Metcalf's metal work is wrought entirely by hand rather than cast. Pellicer's paintings on *amate* (bark paper used in pre-Hispanic Mexico and still available today) are custom-framed in copper. *LEFT:* The spacious estate of American sculptor James Metcalf and his wife, Mexican artist Ana Pellicer, is situated in the copper-making village of Santa Clara del Cobre, Michoacán. In a sculpture garden displaying his work, Metcalf has left the surrounding adobe wall its natural color. Not surprisingly, Metcalf uses copper in his hand-hammered sculptures. *OPPOSITE:* Michoacán is a forested, mountainous area where lumber is plentiful. When the two artists completed the house in 1990, they chose to leave the wood paneling in its natural state. The copper vase in the foreground is from the school/workshop they established in Santa Clara del Cobre.

RIGHT: A guest room in American photographer Deborah Turbeville's highly personalized home in the Mexican mountains is sumptuously furnished. An antique wrought iron poster bed is swathed in artistically tinted natural linen. A collection of antiques are clustered on the colonial style fireplace. The walls are subtly color-washed and ragged by a local artisan. With the help of Mexican designer Patricia O'Gorman, the original house was remodeled over a period of four years. *ABOVE:* Turbeville's sixteen-foot-high living room walls are artfully washed in a midnight blue. Built-in bookcases flank the custom-made fireplace. An array of antiques and ornamental objects decorates the mantel.

LEFT: Rose-colored walls enhance the warmth and charm of the large, eat-in kitchen. A windowed cupola above floods the room with natural daylight. Hanging *retablos* and an assortment of folk art fill the ledges, counters, and high walls. In winter, the fireplace creates a cozy center. *BELOW:* Hanging from the doors of an antique *ropero* (wardrobe) is a collage of found treasures, including vintage ex-votos and a copy of a colonial-style lock in the shape of a violin. The aged, chipped, blue-painted surface of the *ropero* was left as it was.

CHAPTER

9

CASA DE LA TORRE

LEFT: A patio area leading up to the front door is lined with plant-filled *nichos* (niches) and plants in antique molasses jars. The deep, oxblood-red exterior walls make Casa de la Torre's massive proportions seem more human in scale. *OPPOSITE:* A view of the tower building, now surrounded by mature planting, for which the Casa de la Torre (House of the Tower) is named.

ONCE A PART OF THE BISHOP OF CUERNAVACA'S residence, the Casa de la Torre was bought and renovated by the American artist and collector Robert Brady (1928-1986). After he died, the remarkable house, with its collection of more than a thousand pieces of art, was opened to the public. It is now known as the Brady Museum. ❀

RIGHT: Masks from Guerrero and ceramics from Michoacán are among the objects on display in a sitting room near the entry. BOTTOM: Large ceramic angels from San Agustín de las Flores, Guerrero, line up in front of the window of the intimate sitting room.

CHAPTER

10

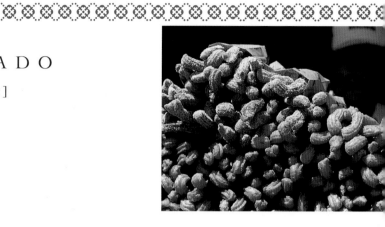

EL MERCADO

[The Market]

ABOVE: A pile of *churros*, Mexican donuts, almost obscures its seller. OPPOSITE: Neat piles of green *nopal* cactus, their thorns carefully removed, glisten on top of shiny turquoise plastic.

AN AMERICAN MARKET IS A DEPOPULATED assembly of shelves. A Mexican market is spectacle. A visit to an American supermarket is dispatched with—items checked off against a list, merchandise packed into the car, a solitary car ride home. A visit to *el mercado* by comparison might provide an entire day's entertainment, requiring as much time to tell about as it took to visit. ✽ *"¡Escójale!"* cry the sellers. ("Choose one!") *"¡Barato!"* ("Cheap!") Sight, sound, taste, smell: the Mexican market is a total immersion. Here, the full color palate is unleashed. Zesty *licuados* (blended fruit drinks), bubbling *carnitas* (pork), symmetrically piled arrangements of foods whose very names are colors: orange, lime, melon, papaya, squash, greens. Women in aprons from the nearby villages proffer fresh tortillas, *nopales* (cactus), *salsa*. ✽ The abundant Aztec marketplaces the first Spaniards describe were not so different from today's great emporia in Guadalajara and Mexico City, or the sprawling provincial markets or village open-air stalls with their few items spread on blankets in the bright sun. Not merely foods of all kinds but anything one might desire can be found in *el mercado*: clothes, baskets, furniture, household items, cassettes, curative herbs, and charms. ✽ *"¡Escójale!"* How can anyone be depressed at a Mexican market? ✽

THESE PAGES: Every stand in a Mexican market—whether selling food, flowers, fabric, or supplies—spills over with color. Even the lowly bucket comes in a choice of bright, cheerful colors.

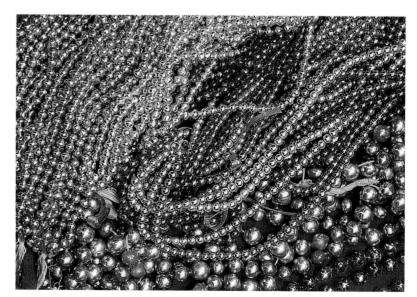

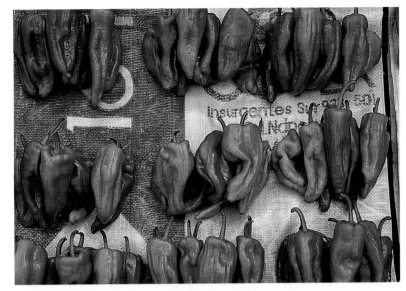

LEFT: Pan dulces (sweet pastries) of *papier mâché* are shaped and colored to closely resemble the real thing. BELOW: Gorditas—thick stuffable tortillas for sale in the market—sit on an embroidered cloth. Both are made by the same woman.

LEFT: A young woman on Janitzio Island in Lake Pátzcuaro, Michoacán, makes tortillas by hand. Her blue and white blouse and skirt are native to the island. *BELOW:* Homemade sweets of candied yams, coconut, nuts, and seeds are for sale at little outdoor stands, or from walking vendors bearing them in baskets. *OPPOSITE, TOP:* Piles of tiny Lake Pátzcuaro whitefish for sale, surrounded by copper pots to cook them in *OPPOSITE, BOTTOM:* A fish restaurant on Janitzio Island. Fish, and the act of fishing, are common design motifs in the textiles, ceramics, and jewelry of the area.

LEFT: A stand in front of a church sells decorations made of palm leaves the Sunday before Easter. After being blessed, the palm leaves are hung inside the home until the next year. *LEFT, BOTTOM:* A street vendor sells brilliantly dyed feather dusters. The long ones are used to clean high-ceilinged Mexican homes. *BELOW:* A woman sits surrounded by her wares in the Uruapan market. The pottery is painted with a pattern of brightly colored flowers.

ABOVE: An array of dramatic terra-cotta jars from Cochucho, Michoacán. The jars come in sizes up to more than three feet tall. Rounded on the bottom, they are placed on padded straw rings for stability.
LEFT: Michoacán women sell their ceramic wares at the Uruapan crafts fair on Palm Sunday, dressed in velvet and lace aprons and brightly embroidered blouses.

CHAPTER

11

WOOD

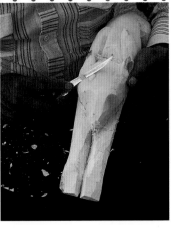

THROUGHOUT THE COLONIAL ERA, Mexico's towns and haciendas used wood liberally. Huge *vigas* (beams) anchored the roofs of the public buildings and grand homes. Tables and chairs were hewn out of pine, oak, and mesquite. Furniture ranged from the complex woven wood-and-leather *equipal* chairs and tables to massive oak dining room tables that seated more than thirty people. ❀ Today, Mexico pays the price for this lavish use of wood. Deforestation has altered agricultural conditions, and has forced an ever-greater reliance on other fabricating materials—cement, iron, plastic. The great *coaba* (mahogany) forests of Chiapas are depleted, victims of overharvesting. Old wood doors, *baúls* (chests), beds, and armoires from the colonial era survive now only as expensive antiques. The delightful wood *castillos* (castles), once part of every pyrotechnic display at *fiestas*, have been curtailed or replaced by plastic versions. ❀ Fortunately, woodworking survives, though on a smaller scale, in the form of handcarved combs, spoons, chocolate whisks, canes, and figurines; exquisite lacquered trays, boxes, and chests from Olinalá, Guerrero; handcarved wooden animals from Coyotepec or Oaxaca; painted wooden toys and games of endless variety—a testimony to the craftspeople who devoutly keep these arts alive. ❀

ABOVE: These unpainted hand-carved figures of dancing *viejitos* (little old men) are made in the village of Tzintzuntzan, Michoacán. LEFT: Carved pine items of all descriptions are available in Tzintzuntzan.

ABOVE: Maestro Manuel Jiménez of Arrazola, Oaxaca, began carving wooden animals in the 1950s. Though others carve and paint wooden animals in the area, Jiménez' curiously animated creatures remain unique, and are avidly collected. *LEFT:* Acrylic paint is being applied to contemporary wooden animals. Acrylics were first developed in Mexico for use in mural painting.

ABOVE: A wedding chest from Oaxaca on its matching table. A souvenir tin *nicho* on top of the chest contains a saint from Oaxaca. An all-night candle bears the image of the Virgin of Guadalupe. RIGHT: Michoacán is a forested region known for its wood products. Here, carved wooden salad servers and a chocolate whisk lean against floral-patterned bowls.

ABOVE: A selection of masks made by Maestro Juan Orta Castillo of Tocuaro, Michoacán. LEFT: The maestro carving a new mask out of a tree trunk. Castillo has exhibited his work and demonstrated his mask-making techniques in Europe and the United States.

LEFT: A fanciful assembly of minutely decorated carved wooden animals typical of Coyotepec. The armadillos have heads made separately, connected in such a way that they bob up and down at the slightest touch. *ABOVE:* An assortment of Coyotepec animals, angels, and other figures against a bright purple wall. The blue-clad angel with the upright wings is the work of Epifanio Fuentes. *RIGHT:* Maestro Epifanio Fuentes, a specialty woodcarver known for his angels, is shown here in his *taller* (workshop) in Coyotepec, Oaxaca.

CHAPTER

12

METAL

METAL SKILLS EXISTED IN MESOAMERICA long before the Europeans came, and amazed the conquistadors when they beheld them. Bernal Díaz del Castillo wrote how Cortés told Montezuma "to bring out the gifts he had brought. The first was a wheel made of very fine gold as big as a cartwheel… another large wheel of silver like the moon, and ten necklaces of prime workmanship… all of very fine gold." Aztec artisans knew the lost-wax method, which took a knowledge of metallurgy and manual dexterity. They made axes, bells, tongs, and other objects from copper as well. ❀ Mexican gold and silver filled European coffers for centuries—Guanajuato's mines alone produced close to a third of the world's silver well into the 1800s. Today, Mexican artisans work in copper, gold, iron, tin, lead, and steel. The Guanajuato and Taxco mines still produce commercial silver, from which beautiful jewelry is made. Santa Clara del Cobre's marvelous hand-hammered copperware is celebrated in Mexico and abroad. Earrings and other jewelry are fashioned of silver; so are ornamental gift and household items—and the little *milagros* (miracles) purchased by millions of Mexicans and pinned to saints' robes in churches to ask for divine intercession. ❀

ABOVE: Hand-beaten copperware for the kitchen is expertly made in the workshop of James Metcalf and Anna Pellicer in Santa Clara del Cobre, Michoacán. *OPPOSITE:* Tiny *milagros* (miracles), usually made of "junk silver," are common in Mexican churches or sacred sites. Available in the shapes of people, animals, body parts, cars, and other images from life, they are offered as prayer or thanks to favorite saints.

RIGHT: Two elaborate tin candleholders from San Miguel de Allende. The left one is in the shape of a sacred heart. The other has a glass and pierced-tin compartment for the candle. The antique copper-like patina is applied with a chemical.

FAR LEFT: An assortment of metal and glass lamps from the colonial period hang on a wall inside the entrance of La Hacienda de Cortés in Cuernavaca, once the conqueror's private dwelling and now a popular hotel and restaurant. *LEFT:* Colorful, inexpensive tin ornaments made in San Miguel de Allende. Similar types exist in Oaxaca. The brightness of the tin shines through the transparent colors. *BELOW:* Silver earrings from a private collection of traditional *mestizo* (originally from Spain but integrated into native culture) jewelry.

LEFT: El Portón, a store and workshop in Santa Clara del Cobre, Michoacán, where visitors can observe copper objects being forged by hand. BELOW: Three beautiful heavy copper vases created in the Metcalf *atelier* in Santa Clara del Cobre. The school/workshop is dedicated to teaching and maintaining a high level of copper-making.

ABOVE: An award-winning copper piece on display in the Santa Clara del Cobre museum shows the quality and breadth of design in the local workshops. *RIGHT:* Copperware has been made in Santa Clara del Cobre since colonial times. Today, most of the town helps produce old and new styles of hand-hammered copper items.

THESE PAGES: Wrought iron and cast bronze exterior accessories—window guards, door knockers, railings—add charm and practical decorative elements to buildings throughout Mexico.

CONTEMPORARY
ARCHITECTURE

MEXICO'S CONTEMPORARY PERIOD commenced with the end of the 1910 Revolution. Spearheading the new epoch, visionary Guadalajara-born architect Luis Barragán began plumbing the Moorish sources of Spanish architecture—the garden, the fountain, the court-yard, the wall—and bringing them forward in a new way. He shed the ornamen-tation and paraphernalia of the *haciendas* the ruling class had occupied in favor of high walls, lean lines, and shapes echoing both the emerging European Bauhaus and the austere, silent monumentality of pre-Hispanic temples and cities. Barragán added to all this a love for the Mexican vernacular—the fiestas and foods and colors and objects one sees in daily life. The result was a new language of light, color, and space. ❀ The influence of Barragán's work continues today, notably in the work of Ricardo Legoretta, and among scores of younger archi-tects such as Juan Carlos Valdes. One sees echoes of Barragán too in the Mexican home of San Francisco architects Cathi and Steven House, and in Oaxaca's soft, monochromatic Casa Olguin. ❀

ABOVE: Ricardo Legoretta, who has carried on the Barragán tradition of brilliantly col-ored geometric simplicity, designed the El Camino Real Hotel in Mexico City. Here he juxtaposes a yellow wall with a *rosa mexicana* "fence," blocking off the street while letting in light onto the fountain in the foreground. *OPPOSITE:* An interior foun-tain in the El Camino Real Hotel, setting blue water against a deep blue wall, forms an oasis of serenity in the midst of the bustling metropolis.

LEFT, TOP TO BOTTOM: Interior of the Gálvez house, looking out at the fountain. The pink cement and glass walls merge and amplify inner and outer spaces; walls of *rosa mexicana* soften and color the contemporary dining room of the Gálvez house; a thick partition separates the exterior entrance from an interior-facing fountain. The drainspout design is an abstraction of a type commonly found on hacienda walls. *OPPOSITE:* The Gálvez house by Luis Barragán. The vivid pink wall color *(rosa mexicana)* is a favorite in Mexico. Huge terra-cotta *pulque* (alcoholic cactus drink) jars are grouped together for dramatic effect.

LEFT: The breakfast room wall of this contemporary home by architect Juan Carlos Valdes is rag-painted red over orange, using dry pigments mixed with *cal* (slaked lime whitewash). *OPPOSITE:* Valdes remodeled a home for the Reinhart family much in the manner of Luis Barragán. The large unadorned walls painted in primary colors pay homage to the spirit of that great architect.

ABOVE: In front of the deep blue wall at the far end, a stairway descends to a lower level. The red sculpted square niche echoes the shape of the custom wrought iron railing in front of it. *LEFT:* This outdoor passageway of the Reinhart home vibrates with bright planes of color, accentuated by bold objects from the family's extensive art collection.

ABOVE: Large, earth-toned geometric shapes are lit by skylights. Locally made unpainted furniture and objects blend with the monochromatic setting. *OPPOSITE, TOP LEFT:* A serene location in the valley of Oaxaca is the setting for Mari and Guillermo Olguin's home. The outer walls and roof tiles use the materials and tones of the surrounding earth, as the house interior does. *OPPOSITE, BOTTOM LEFT:* Con-temporary artworks stand out against the iron oxide-colored wall. The fruit appears sumptuous in contrast to the plain wooden bowl. *OPPOSITE, TOP RIGHT:* A Tarahumara ladder from Chihuahua leans against a wall in a two-toned corner of Casa Olguin. *OPPOSITE, BOTTOM RIGHT:* Straw-toned *sombreros* (hats), carved out of wood and left unvarnished, are part of the contemporary art collection at Casa Olguin.

ABOVE, TOP: View of the courtyard in the Mexican home built by San Francisco architects Cathi and Steven House. The spiral designs on the ground, inspired by Mayan glyphs, use river rock of different colors. The rose-colored kitchen serves the patio and the interior dining area. **ABOVE:** The House's guest room is lit by a skylight built into a brick *boveda* (vaulted) ceiling. The beds and other furnishings were designed by Cathi House and are handmade to order.

ABOVE: Steven and Cathi House used all local materials in building their home. The hard edges of the polychrome geometric designs are softened by the use of textiles and folk art in every room. The triangular windows let in the light from the street, and additional light enters from small square skylights and the tall glass doors to the courtyard. *OPPOSITE:* Cement stairs leading off the Houses' patio showcase the undulating design of the wrought iron railings.

CHAPTER

14

NICHES & SHELVES

OPPOSITE: Handblown glass stemware lets the light through a kitchen window over the sink in a former *hacienda* in Marfil, Guanajuato. This type of glassware is made in and around Guadalajara, Mexico City, and San Miguel de Allende. *LEFT:* Ceramics sit on a shelf against a *rosa mexicana* wall with a collection of sugar animals made for the Day of the Dead.

RIGHT: The soothing colors of wood and clay on this *repiso* (hanging shelf) blend harmoniously with the earth-toned wall behind. *BELOW:* A *huacal*, a twig crate design from pre-Hispanic times, is used as a shelf to hold a collector's display. The clay bear is from Chiapas, the Ocumicho fantasy bus from Michoacán, and the corn husk figures on the right from Mexico City. *BOTTOM, RIGHT:* A bright blue free-standing *trastero* houses an assortment of dinnerware in the Con Ángel shop in Cuernavaca.

LEFT: An old hand-painted wood *trastero* (shelf for dinnerware) is laden with mugs from Tonalá, dishes from Morelia, bowls from Pantoja, pastel glazed accessory pieces from Guanajuato, a glass pitcher and cups from Mexico City, and cobalt blue glasses from San Miguel de Allende. Animal-shaped wood bowls from Ixtapán de la Sal sit on kitchen counters covered in tiles from Dolores Hidalgo.

129

ABOVE: Colonial-style accessories cluster on the shelf of a room in Casa Quinta Quebrada. Shiny blue and white Talavera-style ceramic pieces catch the light from the many lit candles.

FAR, LEFT: A rare sixteenth-century Virgin stands on a *repiso* (hanging shelf). Serene in countenance, she bestows her blessings on the home. LEFT: An outdoor *nicho* (niche) built into the stone staircase of a patio in San Miguel de Allende. The Virgin of Guadalupe candleholder is made of unglazed clay and stands 27 inches high. BELOW: A *nicho* built into the thick adobe wall of an ex-convent in Oaxaca, now the El Camino Real Hotel. The current owners have allowed traces of color from earlier epochs to remain. Candles and a statue of a saint complete the picture. BELOW, LEFT: A statue of *San Miguel* (Saint Michael) presides over the deep ocher dining room of Casa Luna, a bed-and-breakfast in San Miguel de Allende. Palm Sunday decorations lie at the saint's feet.

131

CHAPTER

15

CHARMING INNS & HOTELS

OPPOSITE: Rancho La Puerta in Baja California, a luxury spa hidden among palms, caters to guests from both sides of the border. *LEFT:* A quiet courtyard in Oaxaca's El Camino Real Hotel.

LEFT: Hotel Las Mañanitas, in the historic center of Cuernavaca, has long had a reputation for elegant surroundings, good food, and excellent service. Peacocks roam freely across the lawns and around the pool. *ABOVE AND BELOW:* The Camino Real Hotel in the city of Oaxaca is located in a former convent built in the sixteenth century. Artfully restored and providing every amenity, it offers a soothing refuge from the outside world.

OPPOSITE, TOP: The Villa Montaña, in Morelia is one of the most elegant hotels in Mexico. It is set on extensive, beautifully landscaped ground, and each suite is individually decorated. *OPPOSITE, BOTTOM:* A courtyard view of the Casa de Sierra Nevada Hotel en el Parque, recently opened on a historic site near San Miguel de Allende's Juárez Park.

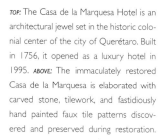

TOP: The Casa de la Marquesa Hotel is an architectural jewel set in the historic colonial center of the city of Querétaro. Built in 1756, it opened as a luxury hotel in 1995. *ABOVE:* The immaculately restored Casa de la Marquesa is elaborated with carved stone, tilework, and fastidiously hand painted faux tile patterns discovered and preserved during restoration.

ABOVE, RIGHT: The private chapel features a stained glass Virgin of Guadalupe. *RIGHT:* The Casa de la Marquesa's huge crystal chandelier is in proportion to the hotel lobby's two-story ceiling. Notable aspects of the building are the iron grillwork, the Moorish architectural details, and the use of color and texture in Talavera tiles and paint.

LEFT: Las Alamandas lies on a hidden stretch of Pacific coast south of Puerto Vallarta. Soft ocean breezes cool a garden of cactus and palms. *ABOVE:* The swimming pool of Cuernavaca's Hotel Hacienda de Cortés is constructed around columns belonging to the original structure. Built in the sixteenth century to house Mexico's conqueror, it has been a hotel since 1981.

CHAPTER

16

TWO BED-AND-BREAKFASTS

OPPOSITE: Deep ocher walls lend a welcoming atmosphere to the dining room of Casa Luna, a bed-and-breakfast in San Miguel de Allende. At Casa Luna—opened in 1996 by Diane Kushner, an American from Marin County, California—each room or suite is a unique experience. *LEFT:* A spacious bedroom in a suite with its own fireplace. The room is painted in the colonial manner, with deep red along the *faldón,* the lower parts of the wall, and a border of blue trim separating it from the pale yellow wall above.

ABOVE: A courtyard fountain in Casa Luna, surrounded by abundant potted geraniums, ferns, and climbing vines. The shell-shaped fountain is an often-used colonial architectural detail. *RIGHT:* A *pasillo* (corridor) leads to a rear patio and other guest rooms. The rosy exterior color is uniform throughout the buildings' many shared spaces. *OPPOSITE:* A corner of Casa Luna's eclectic Red Room, with its blue floor, *equipal* leather footstool, antique daybed, and soaring *bóveda* (vaulted) ceiling. A locally made tin and glass lamp hangs from the circular skylight.

ABOVE: The *casita's* jewel-like kitchen in Casa Liza in San Miguel de Allende is fully tiled with Talavera-style tiles from nearby Dolores Hidalgo. The antique mesquite door is hung with *retablos* (ex-votos). The tin lamp was made locally. *TOP, LEFT:* A fruit-laden papaya tree stands in front of a *casita.* The exterior walls have been washed with layers of color. The antique bench was purchased from a local antique shop. *LEFT:* A *casita* bedroom at Casa Liza. The walls are terra-cotta color. The strip of floral design separating the dark border from the main color above is taken from the house of Father Hidalgo, now a museum in Dolores Hidalgo (the town named after him). The lamps are from San Miguel de Allende, while the beds are antique copies made in nearby Atotonilco.

LEFT: A private *casita* on the spacious grounds. The *equipal* table and chairs are from Guadalajara. The colonial-era doors and windows were salvaged from a nearby ex-hacienda.

A RENOVATED HACIENDA

OPPOSITE: The ex-*hacienda* Molina de Agua was built in 1807 near the holy penitent shrine of Atotonilco, in the state of Guanajuato. American designer Marsha Brown and her daughter Kelly purchased the old mill property four years ago and began restoring and updating it. Here, in a corner of the property, deep red provides a beautiful backdrop for the large terra cotta storage jar, the natural leather tones of the saddles, and the unvarnished woods. The huge cross of wood and tin was made in the nineteenth century. *LEFT:* The interior rooms of the reconstructed *hacienda* are designed with antiques and atmospheric touches. Each wall is done in a carefully chosen color, complementing and enhancing the simple beauty of the furnishings.

ABOVE: A spacious library reawakens a sense of life as it must have been in the original *hacienda*. The bookcase, made in Mexico, is a copy of a seventeenth-century one. RIGHT: An antique crucifix hangs over the stairway to the cellar.

LEFT: Sunlight floods into the master suite through antique lace curtains. Folk art mixes with antiques and antique copies. Two old painted chests from Oaxaca are used to store clothing. *BELOW:* A bedroom in ex-*hacienda* Molina de Agua. Maestro Martín Vásquez Robledo painted the walls, including the motif of the blue border—a variation from one in the nearby Atotonilco shrine. The carved wooden bed is nineteenth-century Mexican, as are the paintings. The blue-figured virgin on the far wall is late eighteenth-century from Querétaro.

CHAPTER

18

PATIOS & FOUNTAINS

THE PREVALENCE OF PATIOS AND
fountains in Mexico stems directly from the Hispano-Moorish tradition in Spain
at the time of the Conquest. As Mexican writer Antonio Haas has pointed out,
"the rich irony is that this style of garden so closely coincided with that of the
destroyed Aztec civilization." ❁ Every town in Mexico has a central *plaza* or
jardín—a public patio, in effect. The public fountains one sees throughout the old
towns were in colonial times not a luxury but a necessity—a place for people and
animals to draw water. This patio-and-fountain design was echoed in the private
gardens behind the walls. ❁ "The patio is the heart of all Spanish colonial architecture," Mexican designer Patricia O'Gorman has said. "A fountain or wellhead
is always to be found in the center." Patio and fountain serve as an armature not
only for plants and trees but for tiles, pottery, stonework, grillwork—all the colorful products of Mexican artisanship. In a deeper sense, patio and fountain are
the repository of Mexican inwardness. ❁

ABOVE: The sound of water dripping from
level to level is a cooling sound in a sunny
Oaxacan patio. The potted palms are sil-
houetted against the melon-colored walls.
OPPOSITE: Vibrant magenta bougainvillea
explode with color beside a circular patio
fountain along the Pacific coast. Cement
pathways and stairs are painted in similar
tones throughout Las Alamandas.

RIGHT: A covered central courtyard of an old colonial home, now a restaurant, in the historic center of Querétaro. Tables and chairs are arranged about the fountain. The rag-wiped blue color over a paler blue contrasts pleasantly with the pink limestone surrounding the doors and windows. OPPOSITE, LEFT: Flowering bouganvillea cascades down the wall of an outdoor public fountain. Once the only source of water for the town, public fountains, each of a different design, are found throughout the old center. OPPOSITE, RIGHT: Painted yellow and orange, this fountain brightens up the west wall of a patio.

ABOVE: All the rooms in this spacious colonial home open onto a large courtyard with a classic fountain. The open-air central courtyard brings natural light and air to the rooms, and the fountain supplies water to the potted plants surrounding it. OPPOSITE: A courtyard festooned with potted plants. Wrought iron patio furniture, commonly used in Mexican patios, is made throughout the country.

CHAPTER

19

LIVING OUTDOORS

MEXICAN LIVING IS, BY CHOICE AND necessity, outdoor living. A mostly sub-tropical country, rich in natural elements, Mexico's outdoors provide respite from heat or cold, as well as the pure pleasure of the abundant natural world—whether valley, mountain, desert, or coast. Outdoors is also where Mexico, still an agrarian economy, does much of its work. ❧ The *petate* (straw mat) and blanket were part of Indian ways before the Europeans arrived, as were the outdoor market. The open-air, thatched *palapa* (shelter) and the *hamaca* (hammock) were (and are) common along both coasts. In Aztec Tenochtitlán (site of present-day Mexico City), pleasure-seekers drifted by boat through Xochimilco's great *chinampas* (floating gardens) and canals, just as they do today. ❧ The Spaniards brought the courtyard, the garden, and settlers ready to work the great ranches. Adobe-walled hacienda rooms, cool enough in summer, became icy cold in winter, forcing people out into sunny patios or courtyards to warm themselves. ❧ In town plazas and parks, people sit and chat, teenagers circle, and bands play. In church *atria*, or forecourts, they gather for religious events or festivals. In rivers, streams, waterfalls, hot springs, and swimming pools, they take dips to cool off. The patio, veranda, and garden are as much a part of living as the kitchen, bedroom, and *sala* (living room). ❧

ABOVE: Rose-colored adobe walls surround a small patio. Both the cast aluminum table and chairs and the white market umbrella are made locally. *OPPOSITE:* Yellow, pink, and orange pillows brighten this outdoor veranda in a Pacific coast house near Puerto Vallarta. The built-in seating area is made of tinted cement.

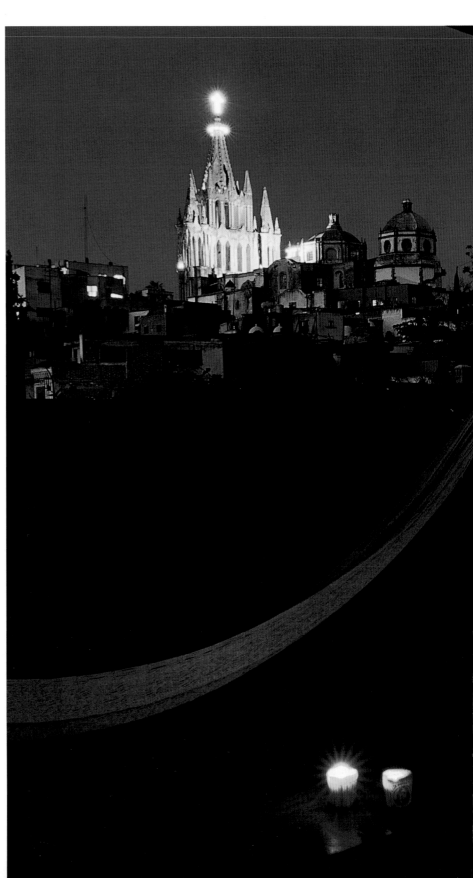

LEFT: Evening on an outdoor rooftop veranda. Candles on a table made from a vintage mesquite door echo the festively lit parish church, as seen through a pillar, a hammock, and the veranda's roof-tile overhang. OPPOSITE, TOP: A covered outdoor lounge in Casa Quinta Quebrada. Sea foam green cotton, loomed in Michoacán, covers leather *equipal* furniture from Jalisco. A deep terra-cotta pigment colors the walls, creating intimacy. The large alcove mirror expands the sense of space by reflecting light from the adjoining outdoor pool terrace. OPPOSITE, MIDDLE: A covered outdoor sitting area displays an eclectic collection of folk art and fabrics against unpainted stone walls. OPPOSITE, BOTTOM: Carved and painted chairs by Roberto Martias from Tilcajete, Oaxaca, sit on a terrace against a bank of tumbling bougainvillea and walls painted *rosa mexicana*.

CHAPTER

20

A TROPICAL FOLLY

OPPOSITE: Situated in the Pacific resort of Puerto Vallarta, the Casa Silver exhibits an eclectic, personalized mix of design influences. *LEFT:* A view of the Pacific from the second-story window of the Casa Silver. The turquoise pool water and blue, green, and white roof tiles echo the colors of the palms and sea beyond.

ABOVE: An old iron bed and other antiques decorate this blue and white room. The *palapa*-style thatched roof lends it an indoor/outdoor feel. RIGHT: Green and blue interior colors lend a cool, fresh feeling to the Casa Silver. The European-looking handpainted wall decoration is reflected in the mirror on the right, doubling the effect. OPPOSITE: An antique bed sits invitingly in an outdoor patio. The lattice wall allows cool sea breezes to waft through.

21

LA COSTA

[The Coast]

COASTAL MEXICO IS A CULTURE OF ITS

own—sensual, humid, extravagant. Along the Gulf of Mexico, where Mayan and Olmec kingdoms once flourished, new resorts and archaeological digs share space with contemporary Mexican towns and the descendants of the early Mayans. The seemingly endless Pacific coast, stretching from Tijuana to the Guatamalan border, includes among its marvels Acapulco's chic resorts and stunning vistas, the exquisite bay of Zihuatanejo, and several imaginative European-built resorts south of Puerto Vallarta. ❀ Lush foliage, tropical rains, turquoise waters. Fresh-caught shrimp, tuna, swordfish. Soft white-sand beaches, quiet inlets, rolling surf. The Mexican coast is paradisical, outsized, extraordinary; architects and builders have responded with innovative ideas. ❀ The *palapa* is an open-air structure of palmetto-thatched roofing supported by a trunk of hardwood. The rediscovery of this indigenous building technique stands at the center of coastal architecture, literally and metaphorically. Add to the *palapa* bright landscaping of palms, cacti, agaves, succulents, intensely colored bougainvillea; clifftop swimming pools of incredible blues, playing off the changing colors of the Pacific; poured concrete structures in audaciously bright colors—and you have a contemporary paradise. ❀

ABOVE: Poolside at Italian builder Gian Franco Brignone's Costa Careyes resort, overlooking the ocean. Carved stone replicas of *equipal*-style chairs offer seating in the shade of an adjacent tree. *OPPOSITE:* Above a sheltered cove on the Costa Careyes south of Puerto Vallarta, the walls of the Casas de las Flores explode with color. The development was created by Italian builder Brignone.

ABOVE: A view across the grounds of Las Alamandas, a secluded Pacific coast resort south of Puerto Vallarta. RIGHT: A pink guest room at Las Alamandas. The thatched pre-Hispanic *palapa* roof is a signature of tropical Mexican architecture.

LEFT: Two buildings at Casa Torre frame the sky beyond. Slatted wood shade areas decorated with terra-cotta pots make artful use of the spaces between the structures. *BELOW:* Terra-cotta planters decorate an upper patio at the Casa Torre. Builder Gian Franco Brignone, blending concrete and *palapa* architecture, has taken advantage of the ocean view. *OPPOSITE:* The Casa Torre on the Costa Careyes fronts a white-sand beach, designed by Mexican architect Diego Villa Señor; a lattice overhang stripes the patio with shadows. These columns are made of *palo de Brasil* wood, which grows along the Pacific coast.

OPPOSITE: Seen from within, the interior structure of a Costa Careyes *palapa* is revealed. Supported by posts of *palo de Brasil* wood, the roof is steeply slanted to shed rain quickly. The leather and wood *equipal* furniture, based on pre-Hispanic designs, is from Jalisco. *LEFT:* A closer look at the interior structure of a *palapa* roof.

OPPOSITE: On a Puerto Vallarta hillside, among thatched roofs, palms, and bougainvillea, water from eight pools *(Ochos Cascadas)* cascades down a terraced hillside, one pool pouring into the next. *ABOVE:* The enchanting Casa Que Canta is built into a steep cliff above Playa La Ropa in the southern coastal Pacific resort of Zihuatanejo. The hotel offers both fresh water and salt-water pools, seen here from the restaurant.

SELECTED BOOKS ON MEXICO

Arts and Crafts of Mexico, Chloë Sayer. (San Francisco: Chronicle Books, 1990)

Casa Mexicana, Tim Street-Porter. (New York: Stewart, Tabori & Chang, 1989)

Convergences, Octavio Paz. (New York: Harcourt Brace Jovanovich, 1987)

Gardens of Mexico, Antonio Haas. (New York: Rizzoli, 1993)

Living Maya, Walter F. Morris, Jr. (New York: Abrams, 1987)

Mexican Homes of Today, Verna Cook Shipway and Warren Shipway. (Stamford, CT: Architectural Book Publishing, 1964)

The Mexican House Old and New, Verna Cook Shipway and Warren Shipway. (Stamford, CT: Architectural Book Publishing, 1960)

Mexico, Antonio Haas. (London: Frederick Muller Limited, 1982)

Patios and Gardens of Mexico, Patricia W. O'Gorman. (Stamford, CT: Architectural Book Publishing, 1979)

Secular and Sacred: Photographs of Mexico, Van Deren Coke, Tony Cohan. (Albuquerque, NM: University of New Mexico Press, 1992)

SELECTED SHOPPER'S GUIDE

USA

ARIZONA

El Paso Imports
4750 N. 16th St.
Phoenix, AZ 85016
(602) 222-9932

CALIFORNIA

Arte de Mexico
1000 Chestnut St.
Burbank, CA 91506
(818) 753-4559

Bazaar del Mundo
2754 Calhoun Street
San Diego, CA 92110
(619) 296-3161

El Paso Imports
913 State Street
Santa Barbara, CA 93103
(805) 963-7530

El Paso Imports
811 University Ave.
Berkeley, CA 94703

The Folk Tree
217 S. Fair Oaks Drive
Pasadena, CA 91105
(818) 795-8733

Galisteo
590 10th St.
San Francisco, CA 94103
(415) 861-5900

La Tienda
San Francisco Mexican Museum
Fort Mason Center, Building D
San Francisco, CA 94123
(415) 202-9703

COLORADO

Zona
107 S. Mill St.
Aspen, CO 81611
(970) 925-3763

DISTRICT OF COLUMBIA

Santa Fe Style
1413 Wisconsin N.W.
Washington, D.C. 20007
(202) 333-3747

FLORIDA

Four Winds Gallery
17 Fillmore
Sarasota, FL 34236
(941) 388-2510

ILLINOIS

Mexican Fine Arts
Center Museum
1852 W. Nineteenth Street
Chicago, IL 60608
(312) 738-1503

NEW MEXICO

Antique Warehouse
530 S. Guadalupe St. #B
Santa Fe, N.M. 87501
(505) 984-1759

El Paso Imports
3500 Central St.
Albuquerque, NM 87106
(505) 265-1160

Pachamama
223 Canyon Road
Santa Fe, NM 87505
(505) 983-4020

NEW YORK

ABC Carpet & Home
888 Broadway
New York, NY 10023
(212) 473-3000

Bazaar Sabado
54 Greene Street
New York, NY 10013
(212) 941-6152

Zona
97 Greene St.
New York, NY 10023
(212) 925-6750

OREGON

Signature Imports
638 S. W. Alder
Portland, OR 97232
(503) 222-5340

TEXAS

Cierra
5502 Burnett Rd.
Austin, TX 79756
(512) 454-8603

Cierra
5154 Broadway
San Antonio, TX 78209
(210) 824-8899

El Paso Imports
4524 McKinney Ave.
Dallas TX 75205
(214) 559-0907

San Antonio Museum of Art
200 W. Jones
San Antonio, TX 78215
(210) 978-8116

Tesoros Trading Co.
209 Congress Avenue
Austin, TX 78701
(512) 479-8377

WASHINGTON

Folk Art Gallery/La Tienda
4138 University Way
N.E. Seattle, WA 98105
(206) 632-1796

Prima Mexico
68 Madison
Seattle, WA 98104
(206) 682-6294

MEXICO

DOLORES HIDALGO

Juan Vasquez B.
(Talavera-style ceramics)
Puebla 56 y 58
Dolores Hidalgo, Guanajuato
tel/fax: (418) 20630

GUADALAJARA

La Casa Canela
Independencia 258
San Pedro Tlaquepaque
Jalisco, 45500
tel: (3) 635-3717/657-1343
fax: (3) 635-1265

Fonart/Tlaquepaque
Avenida Juárez 267B
Jalisco, 91000
tel: (3) 635-5663

GUANAJUATO

Alfareria Tradicional
(Talavera-style ceramics)
Gorky González
Pastita ex Huerta de
Montenegro S/N
tel: (473) 24306
tel/fax: (473) 20090

Fonart/Casa del Conde
de la Valenciana
Km 5 Carr.
Guanajuato-Dolores Hidalgo
La Valenciana, Guanajuato
tel/fax: (473) 22550

MEXICO CITY

Fonart/ Main Office
Avenida Patriotismo 691
Mixcoac, Mexico 03910
tel: 598-1666/598-5552
fax: 598-4262/563-8840

Fonart (Fondo Nacional Para
el Fomento de las Artesanias)
Avenida Juárez 89
Mexico, D.F.

Flea Market:
Lagunilla Market (Sundays)

OAXACA

La Mano Mágica
M. Alcala 203
Oaxaca 68000
tel/fax: (951) 64275

Fonart/Oaxaca
Manuel M. Bravo 116
Oaxaca 68000
tel: (951) 65764

PÁTZCUARO

Casa de Los Once Patios
(House of Eleven Patios)
Calle Dr. Coss
Pátzcuaro, Michoacán

SAN CRISTÓBAL DE LAS CASAS

Fonart/Calle 28 de Agosto 2-c
Frente al Hotel Casa Mexicana
San Cristobal de las Casa, Chiapas 29200
tel: (967) 84240

SAN MIGUEL DE ALLENDE

Izcuinapan
Canal 42
San Miguel de Allende,
Guanajuato 37700
tel: (415) 20594
fax: (415) 20286

La Calaca
Mesones 93
San Miguel de Allende,
Guanajuato 37700
tel: (415) 23954

Veryka
Zacateros 6-A
San Miguel de Allende,
Guanajuato 37700
tel: (415) 22114

SANTA CLARA DEL COBRE

Museo del Cobre
Calle Morelos
Santa Clara del Cobre,
Michoacán

Galeria Tiamuri
Pino Suárez 110
Santa Clara del Cobre,
Michoacán
tel: (434) 30321
fax: (434) 30136

ACKNOWLEDGMENTS

Our thanks to the many people in Mexico and elsewhere who helped us in ways large and small.
Special thanks to A&I Labs, Dolores Avalos and the Camino Real Hotels, Evita Avery,
Marsha Brown, Gian Franco Brignone and Viviane Dean, Silvia d'Alba,
Eve and Philippe de Reiset of the Villa Montaña Hotel, Sharon Des Jardins, Maureen Earl,
Sara Jane Freymann, Isabel Goldsmith, Steven and Cathi House, Martha Hyder, Alice Dale Kimsey, Liza Kisber,
Dianne Kushner, Las Mañanitas Hotel, Susan LaTempa, Ricardo Legoretta,
Helmut W. Leins of the Villa del Sol, Mary Marsh of El Tecolote Bookstore, Mary Jane Mendoza,
James Metcalf and Ana Pellicer, Milou de Montferrier, Patricia O'Gorman,
Ernesto Ponce de Leon, Patricia Edelen Powers, Jack and Terry Reinhart, Pancho Schiel, "Silver,"
Sam Skidmore, Sally Sloan, Mr. and Mrs. Sprowls, Karen Van Geffen of the Marriot Hotels,
Michael and Adriana Vidargas, and Jonathan Williams of Tesoros Trading Company.
—ML, TC, MT